Liberation Days

Liberation Days

David van Belle

Liberation Days
first published 2016 by
Scirocco Drama
An imprint of J. Gordon Shillingford Publishing Inc.

Scirocco Drama Editor: Glenda MacFarlane
Cover design by Terry Gallagher/Doowah Design Inc.
Cover illustration by Punch & Judy Inc. with photography by David Cooper, for the 2014 world premiere production of Liberation Days at Theatre Calgary.
Author photo by Citrus Photography.
Printed and bound in Canada on 100% post-consumer recycled paper.

We acknowledge the financial support of the Manitoba Arts Council and The Canada Council for the Arts for our publishing program.

Production inquiries should be addressed to:
Playwrights Guild of Canada
401 Richmond Street West, Suite 350
Toronto, Ontario
M5V 3A8
Telephone: 416-703-0201
Fax: 416-703-0059
orders@playwrightsguild.ca

Library and Archives Canada Cataloguing in Publication

van Belle, David, 1971-, author
Liberation days / David van Belle. -- 1st edition.

A play.
ISBN 978-1-927922-21-7 (paperback)

I. Title.

PS8643.A524L53 2016 C812'.6 C2016-900108-3

J. Gordon Shillingford Publishing
P.O. Box 86, RPO Corydon Avenue, Winnipeg, MB Canada R3M 3S3

For Emma and Aaltje and Vanessa and Wren

Characters

Marijke Bos, age 25

Emma de Bruijn, age 27

Alex King, age 22

Miles Cavendish, age 34

Aaltje de Bruijn, age 53

Dominee Herman van Egmond, early 60s

Jan van Egmond, age 30

A Canadian soldier, in his 20s (can be doubled with Jan)

A Note about Language

In scenes where all characters speak Dutch, the scene is carried out in unaccented English, including Marijke's monologues. In scenes where there is a mix of English- and Dutch-speaking characters, the Dutch characters speak in Dutch, unless they are specifically speaking in English (as in the case of Emma and the Dominee, who speak in second-language English to varying degrees of proficiency). Dutch speeches should not be subtitled or translated into English in any way. Following Dutch speeches, English is provided in square brackets for the sake of readability and is not spoken. Small interjections of Dutch are translated in footnotes.

A Note about Video

The premiere production made use of video projections to place the play within a historical context. Its use is indicated throughout the text. This context can be conveyed in ways other than video, but should not slow the production.

Production History

Liberation Days premiered at Theatre Calgary in October and November 2014, in co-production with Western Canada Theatre in Kamloops BC, where it opened in January 2015. Both productions featured the following company:

MARIJKE BOS .... Kelsey Gilker
EMMA de BRUIN .... Lindsay Angell
ALEX KING .... Byron Allen
MILES CAVENDISH .... Garett Ross (Calgary)
Trevor Rueger (Kamloops)
AALTJE de BRUIN .... Valerie Planche
DOMINEE van EGMOND .... Duval Lang
JAN van EGMOND and SOLDIER .... Jonathan Seinen

Directed by Daryl Cloran
Set and Costume Design by Cory Sincennes
Lighting Design by Gerald King
Sound Design by Jonathan Lewis
Video Design by Jamie Nesbitt
Dramaturg: Shari Wattling
Dutch Translation: Dymphny Dronyk
Theatre Calgary Artistic Director: Dennis Garnhum
Western Canada Theatre Artistic Director: Daryl Cloran

Liberation Days was developed with the support of FUSE: The Enbridge New Play Development Program as well as additional support from the Alberta Playwrights' Network, the Alberta Foundation for the Arts and the Canada Council for the Arts.

David van Belle

Born in Amsterdam and raised all over Canada, David van Belle is an Alberta-based director, actor, playwright and theatre deviser. He has been Co-Artistic Director of Ghost River Theatre, an ensemble member of One Yellow Rabbit and playwright-in-residence at Alberta Theatre Projects. Recent works include *The Last Voyage of Donald Crowhurst*, *The Highest Step in the World* (created with Eric Rose for Ghost River Theatre and Alberta Theatre Projects) and *Tomorrow's Child* (co-created with Matthew Waddell and Eric Rose for Ghost River Theatre). His other plays include *BUZZ JOB! The True Story of Cal Cavendish* with Kris Demeanor, *The Invisible Project*, and *Of Fighting Age*, created with Col Cseke, Christopher Duthie and Anton de Groot. David is fascinated by people's lives and the ways in which they live them. He shares a beautiful life with his wife Vanessa and his daughter Wren.

Act I

MAY

Scene 1

Music begins from the string prelude to Beethoven's "Ode to Joy" (chorale version).

MARIJKE: In the little Dutch village where I grew up, nothing ever happened. Boys and girls played in their yards, then went to school for a while, church, twice every Sunday, Sunday School, Christian Boys and Girls Clubs, catechism, Christian Young People's Society. They met and married, they worked hard and made children, and the whole cycle repeated. For hundreds of years.

Until I was twenty. Then everything changed.

Under her speech, the full chorale from "Ode to Joy" bursts in. A bombastic film montage—black and white projections of the destruction of Holland, Stuka dive bombers, Dutch soldiers on bicycles, the bombing of Rotterdam, the German Administration, Jews on the back of a truck, Arthur Seiss-Inquart, the hungerwinter. This film is projected on a suitable item or items within the design of the set, not an external projection screen.

There were strange men.

From just across the border and from a few hundred kilometres away, places like Frankfurt and Leipzig and other little villages like mine, Hanbach, Menz, Bergenhusen.

And things got worse and worse. First we saw things we never thought we'd see. And then we did things we never thought we'd do. And it all happened right in front of us, it happened to us, in our streets, in our village square, in our back yards.

Battle scenes, the marching of Canadian soldiers, combat, bombers.

And then one day, after five years, new men came from a long, long way away. Thousands of kilometres. Places like Vancouver and Montreal and other little villages like mine—Sicamous, Goderich, Stettler. And we thought everything would go back to normal.

But it didn't.

Through the bombast, as the music hits its zenith, we hear the sound of low-flying aircraft, as if one hundred feet up, throughout the theatre. It's deafening. We feel it in our chests.

Scene 2

Lights up on a gramophone, playing the music. As the music plays full blast in the theatre, we see CAVENDISH standing beside the gramophone, eyes closed, in a state of reverie.

After a bit, ALEX enters.

ALEX: Sir? Sir? Captain Cavendish?

Nothing.

Captain Cavendish!

CAVENDISH snaps to, pulls the needle off the record, abruptly. The Beethoven has been covering the sound of blackbirds in full birdsong. They've been hidden by the bombast but now burst forth. A bouquet of birds. It's a wonder we didn't hear them before.

Captain Cavendish.

CAVENDISH: Yes, of course, Alex, ah, Private, yes. It's time. Any questions before we begin?

ALEX: No, sir.

CAVENDISH: All righty then. Let's meet the village.

Travelling sequence, down a village road. CAVENDISH leads the way, ALEX keeps up.

West side this morning, then north of the canal in the afternoon, next week Tuesday east and south with Wednesday morning to clean up any loose ends. Are you getting this?

ALEX: Yes, sir.

He fishes out a notebook and begins scribbling, trying to balance travelling and note-taking at the same time.

They arrive at the walkway to AALTJE and EMMA's house.

CAVENDISH: Identify the need. Match the need to the resource. Organize the connection. We are helpful, we are efficient, we are friendly.

Hair.

ALEX straightens his hair.

Fetching. Me?

ALEX: Very good sir.

The two of them approach the door and knock. Blackbirds continue. AALTJE opens the door.

CAVENDISH: Hello there, ma'am. We're from the regimental command, just over the rise there. We just came by to say hello and introduce ourselves.

Pause, no response from AALTJE.

I'm Captain Miles Cavendish. How do you do.

He extends his hand. She shakes it.

And this is Private King, my aide.

ALEX: How'd you do.

They shake. Silence.

CAVENDISH: We're just checking in, making sure everybody's OK here, are there any medical needs, got a little food in the house by now, you know…

Silence.

So…

Silence.

Everything's OK? Everything's OK then.

Silence.

All righty then. Just thought we'd check in.

They turn to leave down the steps. As they do so, AALTJE calls over her shoulder, back into the house, sharply, a screech, startling them.

AALTJE: Emma!

CAVENDISH: My goodness.

AALTJE: De Tommies zijn hier. [Tommies are here.]

EMMA arrives. She wears a pair of men's shoes. EMMA and AALTJE speak to each other in Dutch. EMMA speaks to CAVENDISH in English.

EMMA: Wie is het? [Who is it?]

AALTJE: Kom op, gebruik dan je Engelse les, zeg iets tegen deze kerels. [C'mon, put those English lessons to use, and talk to these guys.]

EMMA: Yes? Oh! Het is jij! [It's you!]

ALEX: It's you! You remember me?

CAVENDISH: Private. Hi there, we're from the regimental… You speak English?

EMMA: I studied a little.

CAVENDISH: Wonderful. We had hit a rut… We're just stopping by to say hello, to uh, to introduce ourselves, introduce, yes?—

EMMA: —yes introduce—

CAVENDISH: —introduce ourselves—Captain Cavendish, *(Shakes.)* Private King, *(Shakes.)* and see if you needed anything, if everything was all right.

EMMA: *(To AALTJE.)* Hij wil weten of wij iets nodig hebben, hoe het gaat. [He wants to know if we need anything, if everything's all right.]

AALTJE: Of wij iets nodig hebben? Hoe het gaat? [If we need anything? If everything's all right?]

(To CAVENDISH.) Ben je helemaal gek? De helft van de huizen liggen plat. De familie hier naast woont in een schuur, samen met hun varkens, en mijn kind vergaat van de honger. Ze draagt de schoenen van haar vader, die dood is, en er is niks aan te doen. En jij wil weten of wij iets nodig hebben?

[Are you completely crazy? Half the houses are knocked down. There's a family in the barn next door living with the pigs and my kid is still skin and bones. And she's wearing the shoes of her dead father because there's nothing else to do about it. Do we need anything?]

EMMA: *(To CAVENDISH.)* Yes, we're all right.

CAVENDISH: All righty then. We'll be on our way. Thank you for your time, ma'am, ma'am. *(He turns to leave.)*

ALEX: The doorway!

EMMA: Yes!

CAVENDISH: Private.

They leave.

AALTJE: Idioten. [Idiots.]

She leaves.

EMMA: Mannen. [Men.]

Scene 3

The street. ALEX enters. He's on an errand—got a package of documents under his arm. He scans—it's as if he's hoping to run into EMMA on the street. But instead of EMMA, MARIJKE enters and finds him.

MARIJKE: Hey, Joe!

ALEX: Joe?

MARIJKE: Hey, Joe! Whaddya know?

ALEX: What do I know? I don't know. What do I know?

MARIJKE: Cigarette? Chocolate?

ALEX: Sorry.

MARIJKE: Guilders? Guilders for pretty girls?

ALEX: Sorry, haven't got any.

MARIJKE: Nou, dan ben jij niet veel waard, he. [Not much use then, are ya.]

He turns out his pockets.

ALEX: Sorry.

MARIJKE: You are a bum, Joe.

She exits.

EMMA enters from the other side with her shopping bag, en route to stand in line at the grocer's, her ration cards in hand. She blows past ALEX, who runs to catch up to her.

ALEX: Hi! Hello! Hi there.

EMMA: Hallo. Hello.

ALEX: Alex King, Private King.

EMMA: Yes!

ALEX: I saw you. On the day, with the fighting in the village. I saw you for a second through the doorway. In the shed. In your garden. You saw me.

EMMA: Yes, I saw you!

ALEX: You saw me!

EMMA: In the, in the…ground. In the dirt.

ALEX: In the dirt, yes. *(He mimes holding up a rifle.)* Kapow kapow!

EMMA: You have very big teeth.

ALEX: Oh.

EMMA: When you come into town, all of you together down the street. Red hair and big teeth.

ALEX: *(Doffs his cap.)* No red hair.

EMMA: But big teeth.

ALEX: Yeah, I guess. *(Awkward pause.)* Say, they're havin' a kind a get-to-know-ya dance down in the Catholic church hall and it's tomorrow night and I wasn't gonna go but then I run into you and so… Whaddya say we, uh… Do ya wanna, you know… go, with me?

EMMA: Go where?

ALEX: Go. With me. To the dance, at the Catholic church hall. Tomorrow night.

EMMA: No, I'm sorry.

ALEX: Aw c'mon why not? It'll be swell!

Pause. The DOMINEE enters. EMMA clocks him.

EMMA: I go somewhere else tomorrow. With you. Not to the Catholic church.

ALEX: OK! You got it. Anywhere you want.

EMMA: Come to the end of Oranjestraat. Orange Street. Nineteen o'clock. Bring something with you.

ALEX: Bring what?

EMMA: Bring something…nice. For me. I have to go, I have to queue. Oranjestraat, tomorrow, nineteen o' clock.

MARIJKE enters. She and EMMA clock each other, then push past each other. MARIJKE, crosses, dodges the DOMINEE.

DOMINEE: Meisje. Juvrouw Bos. Kom is hier, meisje. [Young lady. Miss Bos. Come here, girl.]

MARIJKE comes over, surreptitiously pulls a cigarette out from behind her ear and hides it.

ALEX: *(Calling after EMMA—this text can overlap with the DOMINEE's previous line.)* What's nice? Like flowers? Flowers? Shit, there's flowers everywhere, stupid.

DOMINEE: Wat is er, meisje? Je zegt niet gedag teggen de Dominee. [What's the matter girl? You don't say hello to the Dominee.]

MARIJKE: Goeie middag Dominee. Good afternoon Dominee.

ALEX exits. DOMINEE takes a moment to look over MARIJKE. Language switches.

DOMINEE: Where are you off to today, girl.

MARIJKE: I'm on my way home.

DOMINEE: I see. But home is this way, correct?

MARIJKE: Yes.

DOMINEE: And the soldiers' billets are that way, yes?

Pause. MARIJKE shrugs.

You wouldn't lie to your Dominee, would you? I baptized you when you were a baby.

MARIJKE: I'm taking the long way.

DOMINEE: I see. That is a very long way home.

MARIJKE shrugs.

Ahah. No words for that. And can you not call me sir, like a civilized girl?

MARIJKE: I'm not a girl.

DOMINEE: I beg your pardon?

MARIJKE: I'm not a girl.

DOMINEE: Are you a woman, then? How old are you?

MARIJKE: Shouldn't you know? You baptized me when I was a baby.

DOMINEE: Watch your smart mouth. You used to be at catechism every Tuesday. You reap what you sow.

MARIJKE: You don't have anything to tell me anymore.

DOMINEE: What did you say?

She exits.

Oh I've got plenty to tell you. Girl. Miss Bos! Come back here!

Scene 4

EMMA unpacks her stash of food. AALTJE is cooking.

EMMA: More flour.

AALTJE: That's good.

EMMA: A whole litre of cooking oil.

AALTJE: Finally.

EMMA: Three of these things. *(She unpacks tins.)*

AALTJE: Corn, again? People dying on the streets of starvation not more than two weeks ago and they give us corn to feed the pigs?

EMMA: Moeder[1], I told you they eat it themselves.

AALTJE: Astonishing. That we could get liberated by a band of corn eaters. Buncha boeren lullen[2]. And that new mayor of ours, introducing Major someone from the Tommies out in the square, and he's from Lake Saskahoochiehoochie or somewhere. How are ya supposed to take that seriously?

---

1 [Mother]
2 [Farmers' dicks]

EMMA: They're not Tommies, I keep telling you.

AALTJE: Hm.

Silence. They work together, briskly, efficiently. Finally:

EMMA: Moe. Moeder. I'm going out tomorrow night.

AALTJE: Where are you going?

EMMA: Out. With a man. One of the soldiers.

Stop. AALTJE stares at EMMA.

AALTJE: So that's it. Forget about who's waiting.

EMMA: Nobody's waiting, Moe. Nobody but me.

AALTJE: Do you even want to live in this village anymore?

EMMA: Moe, it's not like that.

AALTJE: Jongen[3] smiles at you, got the best intentions in the world.

EMMA: Moeder, it's that young man who showed up here yesterday. With the nervous fellow. They were offering their help.

AALTJE: What are you after? You know they're going home. They know it too. They just want a good squirt before they run on up the gangplank and 'goodbye! goodbye!' And then what happens to all the girls waarmee ze fokken[4] while they're here?

EMMA: It's just a visit. He seems like a nice young man.

AALTJE: There are no nice young men! You wanna end up with your head shaved in the streets like your friend Marijke?

EMMA: She's not my friend.

3 [Boy]
4 [They've bred with]

AALTJE: You saw what that mob was like on Liberation Day. And it won't be just the kraut whores this time.

Pause. They go back to work.

He's coming home.

EMMA: Moe! I'm going.

AALTJE: Since you were a child you—

EMMA: I am not a child! I should have my own children—four, five years ago! But instead I'm stuck here, no men, no family, all right? So I'm going to take care of myself!

AALTJE stalks out. EMMA yells after her.

And I'm going out tomorrow night. And… "boogie woogie." That's it.

AALTJE charges back in.

AALTJE: Then you'd better come back with some food at least. Or cigarettes. Or something else we can sell if you're gonna whore yourself out.

Pause.

EMMA: OK.

Pause. They square off. Then AALTJE stalks off again.

AALTJE stalks back on again.

AALTJE: And don't cry to me later when you've thrown everything away for a boy you've just met.

EMMA: I know that I won't.

AALTJE stalks back off, then back on again.

AALTJE: And if you're knocked up you're goin' to the nunnery.

EMMA: Moe!

AALTJE: That's right, I'll send you to the CATHOLICS, Lord help me.

EMMA: I'll do what I want to do.

AALTJE stalks back off, then back on again.

AALTJE: Don't burn the potatoes.

EMMA is about to break in, but AALTJE holds up a finger, menacingly, warning her not to…

AALTJE stalks off.

Pause.

EMMA struggles, holds back a response, then lets it go, cooks. She can't hold it back anymore, so she crosses to the door and flings it open, about to continue the argument. But instead of AALTJE, there's MARIJKE, holding the lid for a milk pail.

EMMA: Oh!

MARIJKE: Hi, Emma.

EMMA: Hello there, Marijke.

MARIJKE: My sister said you forgot the lid for the pail last time you picked up the milk.

EMMA: Isn't the milk her job?

MARIJKE: She's sick in bed.

EMMA: Hm. We're not going to die without that lid if we don't have it for a few days.

MARIJKE: Emma, I thought maybe you and I could—

EMMA: We do have other lids.

Pause.

MARIJKE: Fine. *(She turns to go.)*

EMMA: See you later then.

MARIJKE: *(Turning.)* The war's over. Why can't we just talk about what happened—

EMMA: Sorry? I don't know what you mean.

Pause.

MARIJKE: All right then. *(She goes.)*

Pause.

EMMA: The potatoes! (*They've burned.)* Ah…shit!

Scene 5

ALEX sits at a cramped stool in CAVENDISH's headquarters, a requisitioned house. Typing on a field typewriter, the portable kind, which is set up on a box, that is just a little too short for the task, meaning that his knees are spread wide and get in the way of his elbows. CAVENDISH paces, his jacket off, tie and shirtsleeves loosened, at his best, dictating:

CAVENDISH: And so (comma) gentlemen of the regiment (comma) I leave you with several important points of advice for dealing with the Dutch people (colon).

Remember that you are the representatives of the Empire and that you wear His Majesty's uniform (period).

Be polite and helpful (exclamation mark). Is that a bit much?

ALEX: *(Shrugs.)* Exclamation mark.

CAVENDISH: *(Continuing.)* Remember that some of the Dutch may be near to starvation—and that the organization of food distribution may take time (period).

Did you read about that? Down near Eindhoven, platoon of Americans pull in, starts throwing out loaves of bread like they're the bloody apostles. An old woman got trampled to death. Can you imagine? Living through the whole war only to be undone in the moment of your own liberation by idiocy.

OK. *(ALEX readies.)* Be patient if you find a Dutchman hard to understand (double dash) he is having difficulty too (exclamation mark).

New line new line.

(all caps.) HOWEVER (colon).

Do not forget to leave your billets in as good a condition as you found them (exclamation mark).

Do not catcall, whistle, leer at, grope or approach a Dutch woman in any way that could be seen as disrespectful (exclamation mark). We cannot stress this enough (exclamation mark).

And DO NOT (all caps do not) overdo the drink in public (exclamation mark… exclamation mark! exclamation mark!) *(Sighs.)*

New line new line, signing off, Captain Miles Cavendish, and such and such.

ALEX finishes.

How was that?

ALEX: I liked the part about the billets. It's a good idea.

CAVENDISH: I thought so too. What's next?

ALEX: Dailies, sir.

ALEX feeds a new form into the typewriter. A lazzo of carbon papers—he has to wrestle with it a bit to get it into the typewriter. CAVENDISH watches.

CAVENDISH: Gently.

ALEX finishes, then waits.

What's her name?

ALEX: Emma? I think.

CAVENDISH: Aha. That one with the silent and loud mother. Not bad, exclamation mark!

ALEX: Yup.

CAVENDISH: So? To the dance tonight. It's an excellent mixer for the men and the Dutch population.

ALEX: She doesn't want to go to the dance.

CAVENDISH: Why on earth not?

ALEX: She won't go to the church hall. We're meeting somewhere else.

CAVENDISH: Won't go to the church hall?

ALEX: Right after we're done here.

CAVENDISH: Ah, well then I won't keep you any longer than I need to. Godspeed, Private. *(He pounds his chest like a Roman soldier.)*

All right. Dailies.

ALEX types.

Tomorrow's movie at the Sally Ann Theatre will be *Practically Yours* starring Claudette Colbert and Fred MacMurray (period). Comedy and romance are afoot when a GI's message to his faithful pooch is mistakenly sent to his fiancée…

He turns around at his business to discover that the DOMINEE is in the room, staring at him. He jumps.

My goodness!

DOMINEE: Mister Cavendish, you and I have some things to discuss.

CAVENDISH: Oh, yes?

DOMINEE: Oh yes, oh yes. *(He holds up a white paper.)* Can you tell me about this, Mister Cavendish.

CAVENDISH fixes his uniform.

CAVENDISH: I'm afraid we haven't met. I'm not used to seeing unescorted civilians in my office.

DOMINEE: Herman van Egmond. I am Dominee of the Reformed Church. Does that satisfy you? Yes? Yes? Now can you tell me about this, Mister Cavendish.

CAVENDISH: It appears to be an invitation to our dance.

DOMINEE: In the Catholic church.

CAVENDISH: In…the Catholic church.

DOMINEE: I will be telling my congregation not to attend. And an Elder will be standing outside the entrance too.

CAVENDISH: Does he… He's going to join us?

DOMINEE: He will not be joining you, he will be making sure nobody from my congregation goes into that dance! We will not enter the lair of the papist!

CAVENDISH: Mister van Egmond, I—

DOMINEE: Dominee, if you please.

CAVENDISH: Dominee, I recognize you're upset—

DOMINEE: We will not have won the war if you turn this village into one of your parties of–of Molech, with your–your sexy orgies!

CAVENDISH: Sir.

DOMINEE: I know what goes on in a dance! Mr. Cavendish, I am sure every little village looks like ours to you. But in this village we have lived decently. It has been like that for a very long time. But in a very short time—drunkenness and fornication and dancing and motion pictures!

CAVENDISH: We do the best we can to keep our men under control, but you have to understand, sir, these are young men with nothing much to do. It seemed like a harmless way to keep them… occupied. Sorry. Could have chosen a better word there.

DOMINEE: You are going to cancel this dance.

CAVENDISH: I'm sorry, sir, I don't plan on taking orders from the local minister. I must also appeal to a higher authority.

DOMINEE: You are turning our daughters into Jezebels, and our sons into the sons of Ham playing Negro music. And we do not care to laugh at Noah, naked!

CAVENDISH: Noah!

DOMINEE: I will speak to your boss about this!

CAVENDISH: I suggest you do. His name is Major MacDowell. Tell him everything you've told me. Don't skip a word!

The DOMINEE exits, fuming.

DOMINEE: Ach man, donder op! Verrekte ambtenaar! Net een week hier, en nu al de baas. [Aw man, thunder off! Rotten bureaucrat! Just one week here and now already the boss.]

CAVENDISH: That was like a visit from Moses.

Village bells chime. Suddenly, ALEX bolts upright and checks his watch.

ALEX: Oh, jeez.

He grabs his jacket and sprints from the room.

Running montage—ALEX trying to find his way through town. He asks for directions from various townsfolk, getting lost multiple times.

Orange street? This way? Oranyu… Or… Orange street? OK. Thanks!

Scene 6

EMMA waits at the appointed street corner. She's been exactly on time.

ALEX arrives, breathless.

ALEX: I'm so sorry. I got lost.

EMMA: There are seven hundred people in our village. You already for more than a week, are here.

ALEX: I know, but I can't read the street signs all that well. It's a…it's a challenging language. The harder I tried to get here the further away I got.

Pause. She's quiet.

I really tried to be here on time.

EMMA: Mr. King, I am not like the other Dutch girls, the ones who stand in line outside of the dance so the boys can pick them out like cows.

ALEX: Ho-lee.

Pause.

Ah. I brought you something, uh, something nice.

He rummages in his bag. Pulls out two cans of corn.

I traded a guy to get a second can.

Brief ballet of taking, deciding not to take, then deciding to take the cans from ALEX.

EMMA: Thank you.

ALEX: You're welcome. *(Pause.)* Creamed corn. That's really good. *(Pause.)* Good corn.

Silence. They sit.

So uh. You lived here all your life?

EMMA: Yes.

ALEX: Oh. That's…that's nice.

Silence.

EMMA: Where are you from? In Canada.

ALEX: A little place just outside Rocky Mountain House Alberta.

EMMA: And where is that?

ALEX: It's in the west. Close to the mountains.

EMMA: Canada is pink on the map we have in a book at home.

ALEX: Well, it's white a lot a the year. In the winter and in the spring and in the fall, it's mostly white with a little bit a brown here and there.

EMMA: It's very cold in Canada.

ALEX: Yeah like, like nose stickin' cold. You know? If you've got a runny nose everything freezes in there and…

Pause.

It's very cold.

EMMA: *(Simultaneously.)* It's very cold.

ALEX: And this place is...wet. Wet and brown, too, but with a lot more green. Way more green, all the time. Even when it's winter, in some places.

EMMA: There were here trees before. There and there. In the whole village. We cut them down in the winter.

ALEX: It's a pretty little town, though. With pretty girls, too.

EMMA: Mr. King.

ALEX: Alex.

EMMA: Alex. I am not a girl. Talk straight to me. Yes?

What will you do now when you are finished here?

ALEX: Go home to Rocky and find a job I guess, or maybe see if I can stand another year on my dad's farm. I don't know. I like being a clerk. I didn't expect to be a clerk when I got here. I was a rifleman until we got here and then the company clerk shipped home so they gave the job to me 'cause I took typing with the girls in grade nine—no homework, eh. It's pretty good. Nobody does that in my family. If that doesn't work maybe I can get on with a buddy, building houses.

EMMA: A...a carpenter.

ALEX: Yeah, like a carpenter.

EMMA: Like Jesus.

ALEX: Yeah, like Jesus!

EMMA: Do you go to church?

ALEX: Uh yeah, yeah. I go to church. Memorial Presbyterian in Rocky. Every Sunday. Almost every Sunday.

EMMA: Ah.

ALEX: You guys are real serious about religion around here.

EMMA: It is real serious.

Silence.

ALEX: Did you get your door fixed?

EMMA: Say it again, please?

ALEX: Did you get your door fixed? On your shed. I saw you through the broken door. Kapow kapow.

EMMA: Oh, no. In a few months and we will. If we find woods. We have a, a cloth over it. It's good it's springtime. It's warm.

ALEX: Yeah, it is! It's warm! I thought I would never get warm again.

EMMA: It's good to hear the birds.

ALEX: Isn't it, though? Man, can they sing. They sing all the time here. I just wanna sit and listen. They don't look like much but then they open their beaks and…

EMMA: The sun on your face!

ALEX: Boy, I thought spring was never going to get here.

EMMA: It's good it's springtime. Boy!

He kisses her hard on the lips, a little clumsily.

ALEX: Oh boy.

EMMA: Oh boy.

Pause.

ALEX: So… Do ya wanna go somewhere and—

EMMA: No. Absolutely no.

ALEX: Oh, OK, no problem.

EMMA: I like things to be clear.

ALEX: OK.

EMMA: I have to go now.

ALEX: I'm sorry, I didn't mean to—I don't know how to— Can I see you again?

EMMA: *(Pause.)* Yes.

ALEX: I can bring wood! I'll fix your door.

EMMA: Yes. Come to my house next week. Tuesday. To fix the door.

ALEX: OK. Sure. And maybe we can go for a walk and talk or something.

EMMA: What do you want to talk about?

ALEX: I dunno. Stuff.

EMMA: OK. Next week, Tuesday, we will talk about stuff. Fourteen o'clock.

She begins to leave, then makes sure the coast is clear, doubles back and kisses him.

Like that. That's better.

She exits. Pause. ALEX smiles to himself, then exits.

Scene 7

Late night. MARIJKE is out in the street. The band from the dance plays in the distance. A soldier enters with a bottle of beer.

MARIJKE: Canada! God save de King!

The soldier stumbles over to MARIJKE.

Jeetje, wat stink jij! [Aw, you're ripe, aren't ya.]

Mine good Canada chum yah? You like girls? Good Dutch girls? I like you. Good Dutch girls.

The soldier vomits.

Laat het maar los hoor, vieserik. Jeetje—wat vreten jullie? [Yup, let it all out ya dirty pig. Aw geez, what the hell do you eat?]

Yah, you a chum! You sleepy? Yeah.

She lies him down on the ground and starts rifling through his pockets. Suddenly he grabs her and starts pawing up her dress.

Rustig, jongen, rustig. [Easy there, fella, easy.]

Hey, chum?

Wacht, wacht wacht. [Wait, wait wait.]

He bowls her over onto the ground and climbs on top of her.

No. Stop. Stop.

He reaches under and unbuttons his fly.

Nee. Nee. Nee, dat gaan wij niet … Hou op. Nee. Stop! No. No. No, we're not going to… Stop it. No. Stop it!

She flails at his back, helplessly, then cracks him across the head with his beer bottle, or a rock, or her fist. He collapses on her. She extricates herself, with difficulty.

Rustig aan. Moet je even en dutje doen? He? Ga maar slapen. [Oh, ok. You want a little rest? Huh? You just keep on sleeping.]

She goes through the soldier's pockets.

Prima! En ja hoor! *(Pulls out a package of cigarettes.)* Exports. Je hebt goeie smaak hoor. [Very nice. Aaaand bingo! Exports. You're a man of taste.]

She kicks him in the side, then points to the logo on the package.

Good Canada girl for me, hey?

She whips a Zippo out of her pocket and lights one of the cigarettes, expertly, then strolls away.

Scene 8

Outside EMMA's house. EMMA digs in the garden. ALEX enters.

ALEX: OK. Fence is back up on the coop, so you can keep all your eggs from here on.

EMMA: Thank you, Alex. For everything. The door on the shed. For clearing the ditch.

ALEX: You've got the cleanest gutters in the village, too.

EMMA: It's…good that you help.

ALEX: Better than files. And I like spending my afternoons with you.

EMMA: It's all right that you are here? For two weeks you are helping.

ALEX: The CO likes it when the guys help out in the village. So long as they behave themselves.

EMMA: And you behave yourself?

ALEX: Mostly. You behave yourself?

EMMA: Mostly. I take care of things. I take care of my mother.

ALEX: Seems to me like she can take care of herself all right.

EMMA: She stays at home. I go out for food, for the things that we need. So 'the situation is in hand.' *(It's a phrase she knows.)*

Now you get the weeds out. From there.

ALEX: You guys don't like sitting around much, do you.

EMMA: There's a lot to do. We can work and talk about stuff.

ALEX sets to work.

ALEX: Did you guys have enough to eat last winter?

EMMA: No. The Germans, they stopped our food because we help you in the fall. But you didn't come.

ALEX: Sorry.

EMMA: It is not the fault from you. But we were very hungry. Many people died. I travel a lot to find food. I trade.

ALEX: By yourself?

EMMA: Yes.

ALEX: What happened to your dad?

EMMA: He is sick and he is dead in January.

ALEX: I wondered. I didn't want to ask.

EMMA: And my brother Anton is shot.

ALEX: I'm sorry. What was he shot for?

EMMA: I don't know. They shot him for nothing.

Pause.

Did you shot anyone?

ALEX: I think I did.

A silence. Finally ALEX holds up his hands.

Look at that. The good kinda dirty, is what my dad says on the farm.

EMMA: How long will it be until you go home?

ALEX: Hard to say. Sure hope it's before Christmas. Heck, we thought it was gonna be last Christmas.

Everything's so close together. How are they supposed to grow?

EMMA: That's how you do it.

ALEX: You're the boss.

EMMA: You grow pig corn, we grow like this. OK? I'm the boss.

ALEX: Yeah, you're the boss.

He jostles her, playfully, and they kiss.

AALTJE: *(From within.)* EMMA!

EMMA: Ja, Moe. [Yeah, mom.]

AALTJE: *(Coming out.)* Emma, zorg dat die uien—o hij is weer hier. [Emma, make sure those onions are th—Oh he's here again.]

EMMA: Ik dacht dat ik hem voor het eten zou uitnodigen. [I was thinking of having him in for dinner.]

AALTJE: O dacht je dat? [Oh ya were, were ya?]

EMMA: Het lijkt mij wel zo vriendelijk, Moe. Hij heeft ons al twee weken geholpen en hij is niet eens binnen geweest. [Moe, it's only friendly—he's been helping out for two weeks and hasn't even seen the inside of the house yet.]

AALTJE: En wat denk je dat wij hem aanbieden? Dat vreselijk roze vlees? Oat-koo-zeen[5] toch? Dat kunnen wij niet missen. Jij moet mij niet weer vragen. *(She goes inside.)* [What are we gonna serve him, that weird pink meat? Oat-koo-zeen, right? We can't spare it, don't ask again.]

ALEX: She hates me.

EMMA: No.

ALEX: Oh, I think she does.

EMMA: No, she just…looks out for me.

ALEX: But you have the situation in hand.

EMMA: She doesn't know what it is that you will do. When you go.

Pause.

I like to see Canada. To see your farm.

Silence. ALEX doesn't know what to say.

What do you have on your farm?

ALEX: It's mixed. Grow a few crops, we've got a few head a cattle, some horses.

---

5 Aaltje's mangling of *haute cuisine*

EMMA: You are a cowboy.

ALEX: No, it's more like a farm hand except well yeah actually no I'm a cowboy. That's right.

EMMA: You are a cowboy, and you behave yourself. Mostly.

ALEX: Yeah, I guess. I wasn't ever really a ladies' man.

EMMA: A ladies' man?

ALEX: Not so good with the ladies.

EMMA: Why not? You are handsome.

ALEX: Thanks. And you're a pretty girl. Woman. Sorry. I just never really spent time with a woman. I just don't always know what I'm supposed to do.

EMMA: You take the situation in your hand. Come. Shhh. *(She leads him off.)*

Scene 9

A knocking at the door. AALTJE has her hands deep in bread dough, flour everywhere.

AALTJE: Emma! Who is it? Emma! Emma! Goeie grut[6] girl, where are you?

She answers the door.

Oh!

DOMINEE: Mrs. de Bruijn, hello.

AALTJE: Yes, hello, Dominee.

DOMINEE: I've come at a bad time.

AALTJE: No, not at all, uh, please, please come in.

---

6 [Good crud]

She looks for a way to clean off her hands. Nothing presents itself, so she wipes her hands on her apron and offers the DOMINEE a genteel hand.

Forgive me, I'm a mess. It's this flour that the Swedes sent. I don't know how Swedish women stay clean. It gets everywhere, it's so fine.

DOMINEE: It's a good problem to have after all this time, isn't it.

AALTJE: Can I get you something? I've just got a pot of tea on—no more ersatz. English tea.

DOMINEE: Oh yes, please! But just a quick cup—I've got a long list of visits today.

Pause.

AALTJE: Dominee, I'm at a loss. An utter loss. I'm so embarrassed about Emma. I don't understand how she could give up.

Pause.

DOMINEE: Let's begin with a cup of that English tea, shall we?

AALTJE: Of course.

She bustles off to get it. The DOMINEE looks around the front room. AALTJE returns with a tea service.

AALTJE: Here we go. Alstublieft[7]. The girl, the girl, the girl. If we only had some word. Have you heard anything from Jan?

DOMINEE: The last letter was the one he sent from Berlin through the Red Cross in September. My son was always diligent about sending word. He even managed to get a note to me when the Germans were hauling him away on the truck. Imagine.

7 [As you please]

But so much has happened since September.

AALTJE: I've still got the box of wedding invitations. We can just change the dates when Jan gets home.

DOMINEE: A fine idea. I think people will understand.

AALTJE: I'll try again with her. But she doesn't listen.

DOMINEE: But I haven't come to talk to you about Emma. I've come to talk about you.

Pause.

AALTJE: Me.

DOMINEE drinks his tea.

DOMINEE: Mrs. de Bruijn, I've come to inquire as your Dominee about your walk with the Lord.

Silence.

It's been a rocky path for you over the past year. Things have not gone as we would have wished them to go.

AALTJE: No.

DOMINEE: Last Sunday—you didn't receive the body and the blood of Christ.

Pause.

AALTJE: No.

DOMINEE: And not the last time we celebrated the Lord's Supper either.

AALTJE: No.

DOMINEE: Is there something that is keeping you from the communion of the saints?

AALTJE: No, Dominee, it's nothing. *(Pause.)* I'll partake the next time, I promise.

DOMINEE: But if you are having doubts, perhaps we should talk.

AALTJE: No, Dominee. Everything's fine.

DOMINEE: Mrs. de Bruijn. Aaltje.

AALTJE: Everything's fine.

Pause.

DOMINEE: This is Roelof's sweater, isn't it?

Pause.

AALTJE: Yes.

DOMINEE: Still on its peg.

AALTJE: Yes.

DOMINEE: You know you'll see him again, don't you?

AALTJE: Yes. In the life to come.

DOMINEE: And Anton as well.

AALTJE: *(Pause. She is tearing up.)* Yes.

DOMINEE: In Christ we have that hope.

AALTJE: Yes. I just…

DOMINEE: Yes?

AALTJE: Everything's changed.

DOMINEE: And yet, "I am the Lord, I change not." And He will reign supreme even in this troubled time. We can take comfort in that.

AALTJE: *(She wipes her tears, embarrassed.)* Yes, of course, you're right. You're right, Dominee.

DOMINEE: And so you see, we don't have to be sad or afraid.

AALTJE: Of course, Dominee. Thank you, Dominee.

DOMINEE: Does...does that make things clearer?

AALTJE: Yes, Dominee. Much clearer. Thank you, Dominee.

Silence.

DOMINEE: All right then.

Silence.

I should be going.

AALTJE: Thank you for stopping by, Dominee. Very helpful.

DOMINEE: And you know if there's anything you need to speak to me about...

AALTJE: Yes, Dominee. I will. I will.

An awkward pause.

DOMINEE: All right then. I'll be off.

AALTJE: Thank you for stopping by, Dominee. Very helpful.

The DOMINEE steps outside the door. He is about to turn around and say one more thing to AALTJE, but she has already shut the door. He turns, hesitates, and then puts on his hat and leaves. AALTJE leans against the inside of the door. She begins to cry.

Stupid. *(She smacks her own face.)*

AALTJE remains onstage by the door during the following scene, her face blank, lost in thought.

Scene 10

Sounds and images of Liberation Day—cheering crowds, singing "Oranje Boven". Video of jubilation, people dancing, greeting soldiers.

MARIJKE counts guilders in her 'going out' dress.

MARIJKE: Twenty, forty, sixty, seventy.

"You reap what you sow." If this town had a motto, that's what it would be. It's an idea that happens to be very popular right now. "You reap what you sow." It's a variation on "I told you so." If the whole country had a motto, that's what it would be. "I told you so." It's a motto that makes you feel good, because you only get to say it when you're certain that you're right. And everyone sure loves to say it.

Video sound swells, perhaps a striking image.

Seventy-five, eighty... Eighty-five, ninety. One ten.

For the five years before the Liberation, though, things got a little unclear.

We see EMMA and ALEX, kissing passionately. EMMA pulls off ALEX's shirt.

One-fifteen, one-twenty, one-twenty-five...

Wie zaait zal oogsten. You reap what you sow. But what if you sow wild oats and instead you get a Dutch-perfect lawn?

What if you plant your seeds carefully, tend daily, fertilize, hoe with your schoffel[8], water religiously. What if you've done everything exactly right and still nothing comes up?

---

8 [A Dutch weeding hoe]

Video shifts. We now see footage of Dutch collaborators getting beaten in the streets, then women getting their heads shaved by the mob on Liberation Day.

One-thirty-five, one-forty, one-forty-five…that's one-fifty. Spring moves into summer. May becomes August.

It does. JAN enters from another part of the stage, ragged, with a sack slung over his shoulder. He is tall, gaunt, ashen. He crosses to meet the DOMINEE.

JAN: Va[9]!

DOMINEE: Jan!

JAN: Hey, Va.

DOMINEE: Thank the Lord, you're home! I knew you'd come home! I knew it! Where have you been?

JAN: It's a long story.

DOMINEE: You must be hungry.

JAN: I could use a bite, yes.

DOMINEE: I have some pea soup on the stove. Let me get you some.

JAN: Va, I'm coming right back. I've just got to see Emma or I'm gonna burst. I'll be right back, I promise!

DOMINEE: Jan—

JAN: *(As he exits.)* Save a bowl for her too!

MARIJKE takes her kerchief off. Her head is shaved, raggedly.

---

9 [Dad]

MARIJKE: In 1942 I fell in love with a German boy, who also happened to be a soldier. You never really know how it's going to turn out, do you. Wheat or weeds.

She looks at the pile of guilders.

Two hundred more guilders and I can get out of here.

She gathers the pile.

You reap what you sow.

End of Act I.

Act 1, scene 4: "There are no nice young men!" Emma (Lindsey Angell) and Aaltje (Valerie Planche) argue about the newcomers.

Act 1, scene 6: Alex (Byron Allen) offers Emma (Lindsay Angell) "something nice."

Act 1, scene 8: "You are a cowboy, and you behave yourself." Emma (Lindsay Angell) and Alex (Byron Allen) in the garden.

Act 1, scene 10: "You reap what you sow." Marijke (Kelsey Gilker) hints at what happened on Liberation Day.

Photos: Trudie Lee Photography

Act II

AUGUST

Scene 1

Video montage—emigration cards, posters advertising Canada, illustrations from Karl May western novels. The great, wild land.

MARIJKE enters. She has a page torn out of an atlas—it's been folded, but she opens it up for us.

MARIJKE: Canada is pink. It's big and it's pink. Halifax, Montreal, Ottawa *(She says ott-A-wa),* Winnypeg, Calgary, Vancouver. If I put a map of the Netherlands on this map there would be room for two hundred and thirty of them in Canada.

One day to the port at Hoek van Holland, six days on a boat to Halifax, then take the the train to…

She randomly points at a spot on the map, then reads:

Ma-nee-too-lin. Ma-nee-too-lin Island. Right in the middle of the country.

You could walk for a week and not. Meet. Another. Soul. Out on the land, near the water. Rocks and forests, raging rivers and mountains and…Indians! Live with them and learn their ways. Kill buffalo and use every part.

Do what I want to do.

A male voice calls from offstage: "Hey, Kraut whore!"

(A magic spell.) Ma nee too lin.

She runs off to avoid the confrontation.

Scene 2

ALEX and EMMA in the garden.

ALEX: Bet it feels good to grow stuff again, eh?

EMMA: Yes. To have our own food instead of always with our hand out doing. With you.

ALEX: Aw, I don't mind it.

She begins picking snap peas and feeding them to ALEX.

EMMA: You eat things that you are supposed to eat. No barley pulp, no rotten grain, no tulip bulb.

ALEX: When we were in the Scheldt we liberated this tiny village by the seaside. And the local priest…

EMMA has stopped paying attention. She has spotted JAN, who has stepped in to the edge of the garden. His face lights up as he sees EMMA. She runs into his arms.

EMMA: O mijn Hemel! Ik geloof het niet! Je bent terug! Wanneer ben je terug gekomen? [Hi! Oh thank God! I can't believe it! You're here! When did you get here?]

JAN: Net nu. [Just now.]

EMMA: Niet te geloven! Hoe ben je thuis gekomen? [I can't believe it! How did you get here?]

JAN: Ik heb bijna de hele weg gelopen. [I walked, most of the way.]

EMMA: Helemaal uit Duitsland? [All the way from Germany?]

JAN: Van Berlijn. Ik kon buiten Essen met wat Tommies meerijden, tot net over de grens bij Enschede. [From Berlin. I caught a lift with some Tommies outside of Essen and then rode across the border with them and into Enschede.]

EMMA: Ik wist niet waar je was! Ik wist niet of je nog leefde of… Ik wist helemaal niks. Weet je vader dat je thuis bent? [I didn't know where you were! I didn't know if you were alive or…anything. Does your dad know you're here?]

JAN: Ik kwam net bij hem vandaan. [Just came from there.]

EMMA: Hij moet zo blij zijn. Hij maakte zich zo'n zorg. [He must be over the moon! He was so worried.]

JAN: Je kent m'n vader. [You know my dad.]

Pause.

Wie is die jongen? [Who's the boy?]

EMMA: Dit is Alex—hij is een soldaat. Een Canadees. [This is Alex—he's a soldier. A Canadian.]

JAN: Ja, dat kan ik zien. [Yes, that much I can tell.]

ALEX has been standing around, awkwardly. He approaches.

ALEX: Hi there. Alex King. Emma's boyfriend.

EMMA: Jan doesn't speak English. Jan, dit is Alex King. Hij is een vriend. [Jan, this is Alex King. He's a friend.]

JAN: *(Hesitates, then takes ALEX's hand.)* Aangenaam, Jan van Egmond. Ik ben de verloofde van Emma. [Sir. Jan van Egmond. I'm Emma's fiancé.]

EMMA: Alex, this is Jan van Egmond. He is an old chum.

ALEX: Hello.

JAN: Hallo. [Hello.]

An awkward pause.

EMMA: Alex is een klerk. Hij ... hij organiseerd dingen bij hun hoofdkwartier. [Alex is a clerk. He...he organizes things at their headquarters.]

JAN: Veel Canadezen in Nederland. All deze jongens. Zodra ik de grens over was, waren het alleen maar Canadezen, Canadezen, Canadezen. Maar ik heb geen een in Duitsland gezien. Hebben ze besloten bij de grens te stoppen?

[Lots of Canadians in the Netherlands. All these boys. As soon as I crossed the border, it's all Canadians, Canadians, Canadians. I didn't see any in Germany, though. Did they decide to stop at the border?]

EMMA: Dat zou ik niet weten... [I wouldn't know...]

Pause.

ALEX: Well, I should be going. One of the NCOs got drunk on some farmer's homebrew last weekend and hit a pig, so they've got pork roast going for chow tonight.

EMMA: Alex, I'm sorry, we talk in Dutch and—

ALEX: Aw it's all right. You haven't seen each other in a while. I get it.

Studies JAN.

Yeah, I get it.

ALEX hesitates, as if he wants something more from EMMA.

OK then.

He begins to leave.

EMMA: Alex!

ALEX: Yeah?

EMMA: The tins with the key on the side, the, the cow.

ALEX: Corned beef?

EMMA: Yes, corn beef. It was very good. Very…tasty. Thank you.

ALEX: Glad you liked it.

EMMA: Thank you, Alex.

ALEX: See ya.

JAN: *(In English.)* See ya.

ALEX leaves. A silence between JAN and EMMA.

EMMA: He's been very good to my family.

JAN: Has he.

EMMA: He's brought food, chocolate, cigarettes. He's handy—he helps fix the damage to the house.

JAN: How old is he? Eighteen? Nineteen?

EMMA: He'll be twenty-three in December.

JAN: Got his birthday on the calendar in the WC?

EMMA: It's nothing, nothing for you to worry about. He's a friendly boy. He's going home in a few weeks.

Pause.

JAN: Look at this garden! Potatoes are taking over as always. Sun's shining down like nothing's changed. I sweat like an otter on the way over here.

EMMA: It must have been quite a walk.

JAN: Five hundred kilometres. Most of the way through Germany. Look at these feet!

EMMA: Jan… What… I didn't know what happened to you. Where have you been since May? Why didn't you come home?

JAN: There's no order in Germany. It's like a layer of hell—the Americans put me in a camp. It took me forever to convince them that I was a Dutch citizen and not a kraut fleeing the country.

EMMA: We didn't know…

JAN: It's an insane asylum in Germany. Things got bad at the end. Very bad.

EMMA: I can imagine. Same thing here, it—

JAN: No, you couldn't. You just couldn't imagine.

Silence.

JAN: I have a whole stack of letters for you.

He rummages in his bag and pulls out a stack. He places them in her hands.

EMMA: Oh… Thank you.

JAN: One for every week.

Pause.

EMMA: Thank you.

Scene 3

CAVENDISH dictates, as before. He's wearing clean shorts and a white undershirt, with a towel around his neck. ALEX types, this time at a table.

CAVENDISH: In conclusion (comma) let me leave you with three pieces of wisdom (colon).

One (parenthesis). The diligent use of prophylaxis, p-r-o-p-h-y-l-a-x-i-s, is your duty as a member of the Canadian Army (period). Don't bring home something that you'd be ashamed to explain to your mother (period). There are much better souvenirs of Holland to be procured (semicolon) I recommend a wheel of the local cheese (comma) which is excellent and can keep for months (period).

Two (parenthesis). It is inappropriate and downright dangerous (underline dangerous) to partake of local home made liquors (period). These concoctions are not regulated and can produce unpredictable results (period).

(To ALEX.) Poor Swatty says he has no idea how he ended up naked under that pulpit.

Three (parenthesis). Remember that the Black Market (comma) while appealing (comma) can have detrimental effects on the population at large (period). What is a mere cigarette for you equals a day's wage to a Dutchman (period). We came here as liberators (comma) let us remain so (period).

Private. Private King. *(Pause.)* Alex.

ALEX: Huh.

CAVENDISH: You're gone again.

ALEX: Sorry sir.

CAVENDISH: How far did you get?

ALEX: *(Reading back.)* "Naked under that pulpit."

He scans back over what he's typed, then pulls out the carbon sheet and crumples it up.

CAVENDISH: Late night out on the town with your little Dutch girl?

ALEX: No, sir. It was pretty early. Really early, actually.

CAVENDISH: We missed you on the field today in the tug of war—the Highlanders, kilts and all, dragged us through the mud. Everybody was caked with it at the end. What a mess! I cheered madly from the sidelines, but to no avail. Ah well, at least one afternoon of excess energy burned off, and better luck next week against the Princess Pats.

ALEX: I didn't feel much like exercise.

CAVENDISH: Drama in the endive?

ALEX: I don't understand women.

CAVENDISH: They rather elude me as well.

ALEX: She's got a fella. An old fella. He's probably thirty. He just showed up yesterday.

CAVENDISH: Ahh it's a tragedy.

ALEX: You know, sir? She was droppin' hints, like she wanted to go back to Canada with me. Why would she want to get married to me and move halfway across the world if she didn't at least like me?

CAVENDISH: Why wouldn't she be interested in you? You've seen the men around here—there were hardly any here at all when we first rolled in, except for old ones. Older than thirty even.

ALEX: I can't wait to get home. You don't have to second-guess everything anyone says.

CAVENDISH: Alex, I think you will go home a different person from who you were when you left. But you'll be improved. You're lucky. Not everybody gets improved by the experience.

He notices the DOMINEE, who has stood in the room for some time.

Oh! Hello, Dominee. You are by far the quietest clergyman I've ever met.

DOMINEE: Mister Cavendish.

CAVENDISH: No trouble finding your way in again, I see.

(To ALEX.) You can retype that tomorrow morning and we'll finish it off in time for the afternoon posting.

ALEX: Yes sir.

CAVENDISH: Off you go, Alex.

ALEX exits.

(Under his breath.) Private. Private King.

Sir what can I do for you this afternoon.

DOMINEE: I would like to know what your plans are for the care and provision of the children fathered by the men of your regiment.

CAVENDISH: As usual, straight to the steak.

DOMINEE: I see no reason or purpose in beating the bush. Three girls in the village are pregnant, from the families Wilders, van der Meer and van Dijk. Why do we not see your boys in church making honest women of these girls? And why has your army taken no action in these matters?

CAVENDISH: Please, Dominee, have a seat.

The DOMINEE remains standing.

I think you'll find, Dominee, that I'm a reasonable man. Let's speak as equals and address the problem, shall we? Please.

He gestures toward the seat. The DOMINEE hesitates, then sits.

Tea?

DOMINEE: No thank you.

CAVENDISH: Small steps then. Dominee, you're a straightforward man, and I respect that. I will be straightforward, too. The government of Canada has made it clear that we bear no responsibility for illegitimately conceived births, nor do we force our soldiers to do so—

DOMINEE: That is unacceptable. Your men storm about in the town like bull beasts in rut with no thought to the consequences!

CAVENDISH: You have a literary bearing, Dominee. And your English is excellent, sir. Where did you learn to speak it so well?

DOMINEE: I spent two years at seminary in Aberdeen Scotland. I studied Greek, Hebrew, and English.

CAVENDISH: English taught by Scots. That must have been an adventure.

DOMINEE: It was. I am not unknowledgeable about the ways of the young. I did not want to be around the church so like Jonah I went away. I rebelled.

CAVENDISH: You rebelled! You ran off and joined—

DOMINEE: The Presbyterians. After two years of wandering in the wilderness I knew they were not the true church and I returned home. One cannot spend the currency of one's life in one's youth, otherwise there is nothing left.

You are Scots as well, sir?

CAVENDISH: Yes, and a few other things. Mostly Scots.

DOMINEE: Also Presbyterian?

CAVENDISH: Yes. *(Beat.)* And a few other things.

DOMINEE: It is hard to trust a man who believes a few other things.

CAVENDISH: Sir, in our regiment we have Scots, Brits, Indians, French, Ukrainians, Italians…even a few men of German descent. After a while you have to kind of focus on what everybody does the same in order to get along.

DOMINEE: Unfortunately there is one thing that it appears everyone in your regiment does the same!

CAVENDISH: I understand the damage that's happening. I see it, and I recognize that not all of these relationships are even… consensual. But my job, it's like babysitting. There are twenty two hundred young men stationed here and I can't let them get bored or they'll raise hell. But if I try to put them to work in the fields I get hell from the Dutch—we're taking away jobs, and you need jobs right now.

DOMINEE: I might ask you to watch your language, Mr. Cavendish.

CAVENDISH: These are not bad men, most of them at least—they just have finished the job they came out here to do and they want to go home but they can't, not yet. And almost all of them have looked death in the face over the last year. That does something to a boy.

DOMINEE: Boys will be boys, yes, Mr. Cavendish?

CAVENDISH: Yes. And girls will be girls as well. It's a shared problem.

DOMINEE: This is what I have come here to tell you!

CAVENDISH: I'll tell you what, sir. I will make a request that the officers and NCOs of the regiment make a point of attending your service next Sunday, as a peace offering. It will be a good example to the men.

DOMINEE: That is a good start. I shall begin with a meditation on Sodom and Gomorrah. Dutch and English, so no one misses the point.

I shall also ask my congregation to invite the young men over for dinner. We will put the system on a schedule. It will be done decently, and in good order.

CAVENDISH: Fair enough. Let's get the boys out of the bedrooms of the village and into the dining rooms.

DOMINEE: It is a start.

They shake hands.

Where is your uniform?

CAVENDISH: Sport meet out on the greens.

DOMINEE: And?

CAVENDISH: We were defeated by the Highlanders.

DOMINEE: The ruddy Scots.

CAVENDISH: Yes, the ruddy Scots.

DOMINEE: That was the other thing I learned in Aberdeen.

CAVENDISH: What's that?

DOMINEE: Nothing is worn under the kilt.

CAVENDISH: Yes, you're right.

DOMINEE: It's all in perfect condition.

CAVENDISH: It's all…I'm sorry?

DOMINEE: Nothing is WORN under the kilt. It's all in perfect condition.

CAVENDISH: *(Still not getting it.)* Yes, yes indeed.

DOMINEE: Mr. Cavendish.

CAVENDISH: Yes?

DOMINEE: You need to work on your sense of humour. *(Exits.)*

Scene 4

EMMA and JAN, in the countryside.

EMMA: Sneaking away without my mother knowing. It's like being twenty again.

He kisses her. It's easy, familiar. She runs her fingers through his hair.

It's so grey.

JAN: I didn't even know until I got back here.

EMMA: What made it do that, I wonder.

JAN: You still look the same.

They kiss. He begins unbuttoning her dress. She hesitates.

Too soon?

When I'd lie awake at night and listen to the bombers overhead, I thought about being here with you.

He tries again.

EMMA: I just need a few days.

JAN: I was...surprised to see him.

EMMA: It's nothing. Really, nothing.

JAN: All the time I pictured my homecoming—this wasn't quite what I expected.

EMMA: I never did know what to do with your expectations.

JAN: Emmie, just because everything else has been torn down doesn't mean we have to start from scratch.

EMMA: I just need time to get used to the change.

JAN: I want to make a good life with you. We could do it then and we can now. We've been given a second chance.

EMMA: But...

JAN: But?

Emmie, I need you. After everything that happened there were nights in Berlin when I didn't know if I could come home. There were dark days.

EMMA: I had dark days too!

JAN: But you were here, you had...some kind of control over what happened.

EMMA: We didn't! Especially at the end.

JAN: You had your family, you had your friends. I had nobody.

EMMA: People did awful things. Our neighbours! Our friends! People died of starvation.

JAN: You slept in your warm bed every night!

EMMA: What difference does that make? You get to come home to your dad and leave it all behind. My father is dead, from a disease that we would have easily cured if not for the war. It's such a waste! And Anton. Anton! The first student in our family. He was going to be an amazing doctor. Amazing. And more than that—he was a gentle—No one ever had a bad word to say about him. But all of that didn't matter in the end, all that potential, all that preparation. They just picked him up at random and shot him. We weren't even allowed to get his body off the bridge for three days. Everybody had to pass by. Moe ran screaming in the street—I had to drag her back home.

Magpies ate his eyes.

I have to walk across that bridge every day, Jan.

JAN: And what do you want to do about it?

EMMA: I don't know. Go away from here!

JAN: All right, let's go. We'll emigrate to Australia. Or South Africa.

EMMA: But it's more than that. It's you, you're…

Pause.

JAN: I'm what.

EMMA is silent.

I'm what! Am I responsible for what happened to Anton? For what happened to the village? They pointed a gun at me and put me in a truck and took me away, for two years of backbreaking work! I am not responsible!

EMMA: Jan—

JAN: I thought about you every day, every minute, for the last two years. Am I not good enough now?

EMMA: This is not how I wanted to talk to you.

JAN: How are we supposed to talk, then? How can I talk to you?

He grabs hold of her arm.

I don't know how to—

EMMA: Jan!

JAN: Please, Emmie. I need you. I need this.

He tries to kiss her.

EMMA: No, Jan!

JAN: Emmie, please. I need to come home.

EMMA: NO!

She manages to push him off and scrambles away from him. They eye each other.

You stay away from me.

JAN: Emmie, please! I'm sorry—

EMMA: You stay away from me!

JAN: *(Quietly.)* Emmie, please.

EMMA: STAY AWAY.

A tense silence. Then ALEX enters.

ALEX: I thought you might be here. I guess this is a popular spot. Perfect.

EMMA: Alex.

JAN: Geweldig. Precies waar ik binnen kwam. [Perfect. Right where I left off.]

ALEX: Turn around and talk to me. Now.

EMMA: I don't like it to talk to me like that.

The following two speeches together:

ALEX: Yeah, well maybe that's the problem. Maybe I shoulda talked like that a bit more. A little less 'yes ma'am, no ma'am'. Maybe then you'd show me a little respect, instead a showin' me the door like a… like some kind of travelling salesman. Corned beef? Are you even listening to me?

JAN: Het ziet er naar uit dat je liever met een Canadees bent? Sterke jonge mannen. Volle buikjes. Wie zou een Nederlander willen he? Te zwak, te dun. Grijs haar.

[Guess you prefer Canadians, don't you. Strong young men. Full bellies. Who wants a Dutchman anyway. Too weak, too skinny. Grey hair.]

EMMA: Jan.

JAN: Nou. Ik wens jullie het beste. [Well, all the best to you both, then.]

JAN exits.

EMMA: Jan!

ALEX: I got a few things to say to you.

EMMA: I don't like to see you like this.

ALEX: Don't like to? Too friggin' bad. I'm here. I'm like this. This is what I'm like.

EMMA: I don't like it.

ALEX: Well, you don't like the other me either now do ya.

EMMA: That's not true.

ALEX: Second your old boyfriend rolls into town I'm out on my ass, right? Some girlfriend you turned out to be.

I didn't have to come here, you know. I'm a farm worker. An essential worker. I chose to come here. And boy, what a choice. Save a bunch a blond, blue-eyed people from another bunch a blond, blue-eyed people.

EMMA: Alex—

ALEX: What do you even want from me? I work hard for you, I fix up your shed, I—I grab lumber, don't ask me where, and I fix your shed, I got beans, corn, spam, chocolate, cigarettes.

I'm a good man.

But I'm stupid.

EMMA: Alex, I'm sorry—

ALEX: And frankly, looking back on the whole thing, I'd a just a soon stayed home.

Simple. Easy.

Wouldn't freeze my feet. Stay dry most a the time instead a my socks rotting off.

Wouldna seen no one with his eye shot out of his socket. Head cracked open.

Wouldna seen a guy tryin' to sell a date with his wife to the soldiers. What's wrong with you people?

There's a few things I coulda gone without seeing.

And I sure as shit coulda gone without seeing you.

Pause. EMMA begins to cry.

Aw, don't, don't don't. I can't tell you anything when you do that.

EMMA: Alex, I'm pregnant. *(Beat.)* From you.

ALEX hesitates, then bolts.

Scene 5

JAN sits with a bottle of jenever (Dutch gin) at the table. Papers and books are scattered about. He does a drunken shot.

DOMINEE enters.

DOMINEE: It's a little early to be drinking, isn't it? I was saving that.

JAN: For me! It's my homecoming!

DOMINEE: Jenever is meant to be drunk a glass at a time, on special occasions. Not guzzled like a gypsy.

JAN: It is a special occasion! Let us drink and be merry: for this my son was dead and is alive again; he was lost and is found!

DOMINEE takes the bottle and puts it away.

You're no damn fun, Va.

DOMINEE: I should smack you for talking like that.

JAN: Go ahead, smack me. I'm gonna warn you though, I've learned how to hit back.

DOMINEE: We serve the Lord here. I expect you to be civil in this house.

JAN: Civil. Yes, I'll be civil. That's the way things are done around here—decently and in good order. Yes sir, yes…sir.

He stands up and drunkenly salutes the DOMINEE.

Or is it more like this?

He gives a Nazi salute.

DOMINEE: Sit down. I'm ashamed to see you like this.

JAN: God forbid we should be ashamed. You didn't do anything to be ashamed of?

DOMINEE: Certainly not.

JAN: That's not what I heard.

DOMINEE: I've done nothing.

JAN: Never did anything, is the way I heard it. The mayor, Enno the accountant, they stood up to the Krauts and went to Dachau for it. What did you preach about?

(He rummages through the papers.) I found your sermon notes. You never said a word about the war, not a thing.

DOMINEE: The Kingdom of God is always more important than what happens here on earth, war, peace, no matter what. I live my life in pursuit of God's truth. I'm not ashamed of that.

JAN: *(Reading.)* Evening service, June 25, 1942, this was about two weeks after the Jews began being deported if I remember. Sermon topic: Love your neighbour as yourself.

DOMINEE: We had to resist in the ways that we could.

JAN: Did you write letters?

DOMINEE: Yes.

JAN: To the Reichskommissariat? Special delivery to Arthur Seyss-Inquart?

DOMINEE: Of course not.

JAN: To church papers. Endless debate over the finest points of godliness. When people were dying and starving.

DOMINEE: That's not true.

JAN: What did you do when Reuben and Anja Mendelssohn had the windows of their shop smashed? What did you do when they left town on the back of a truck?

And what did I do? A lot of talk about the Kingdom of God, but not a whole lot of talk about the Mendelssohns.

DOMINEE: I am not going to argue theology with a drunk.

JAN: Who taught me the theology, Va? Drunk or sober, it's all in here *(His head.)*.

(He consults a book.) Heidelberg Catechism Question and Answer 5 says that 'We have a natural tendency to hate God and our neighbour.'

Well, that's getting a little more accurate, isn't it. A natural tendency to hate.

DOMINEE: You come back here to a situation you don't understand and pound your gavel. I don't owe you anything.

JAN: Yes you do, God damn it!

DOMINEE: For what, exactly? What do you need me to explain?

JAN: You need to explain what happened, Va. How this happened. Why this happened. You deal with the big questions. That's your job.

DOMINEE: I don't know, Jan.

JAN: You do! You know everything! Or at least you talk like you know everything! You're an insufferable know-it-all. You have always been, for all of my life, an insufferable know-it-all.

DOMINEE: Are you asking me to tell you what was in Hitler's heart?

JAN: Yes, Va. It's this whole thing about this natural tendency to hate God and my neighbour.

DOMINEE: You know this. Original Sin. Adam and Eve.

JAN: A load of shit!

I've seen good people do the worst things to one another. Because they were hungry. Because they were afraid. Or cold and wet.

DOMINEE: God sends strength to those who need him. He was with you in Germany.

JAN: Honestly, Va, don't think he was.

DOMINEE: He was, Jan. I believe it with all my heart.

Pause.

JAN: Va. Something happened in Berlin. I'm... I'm scared to tell you this, Va.

I was sleeping in the main floor of a bombed out row house, just after the war ended. The family was still there in the upper floors, a mother and two daughters, fourteen, fifteen.

One night a platoon of Russian soldiers came by. Drunk.

DOMINEE: Jan, I understand. We all trod rocky paths—

JAN: Please, Va. I need to tell you this. Can I tell you this?

Pause.

DOMINEE: Yes.

JAN: They poured me a little of their booze and we lit a fire in the fireplace and they sang songs.

But then one of them heard a noise from upstairs and he went up to take a look. And he found the mother and the daughters. And he called his buddies up to join him.

They took turns, all night long, seven, eight hours. The girls were screaming, and the mother. They screamed until they couldn't scream any more and then they made these low…inhuman sounds, and then finally, they stopped making noise altogether.

DOMINEE: There was nothing you could… They would have shot you.

JAN: That's not it, Va. I went upstairs too. I took my turn. I didn't care.

DOMINEE: Jan… That was a wicked—

JAN: And actually that's not true—I did care. I could have left, but I didn't. I was glad about it. For everything they did to us.

DOMINEE: On the last day we have to look God in the eye and give him an answer for what we have done.

JAN: Va, listen to me: there is no God. If there was a God, then he left us to fend for ourselves years ago.

And the worst part is, I can't go back. None of us can, now that we know this. We can't go back to church twice on Sundays and Young People's and the pointless, gutless, ridiculous Heidelberg Catechism.

And you know, Va, I want to. I want to go back so badly. If I could just flip a switch and… *(He snaps his fingers.)* I would!

He begins to cry.

I'd sit in that pew and I'd be so happy!

DOMINEE: What happened to you?

JAN: I don't know, Va. I messed it up and Emma doesn't want me. Help me, Va. What do I do?

DOMINEE: I don't know.

JAN: I finally need you to know something. And you don't. Fantastic.

He grabs the bottle and exits.

Scene 6

MARIJKE's house. EMMA enters.

EMMA: Marijke.

MARIJKE: What the hell do you want?

EMMA: I need to pick up the milk.

MARIJKE: Fine.

EMMA: And I…I need to talk to you.

MARIJKE: Well I don't want to talk to you.

EMMA: Marijke please…

MARIJKE exits, returns with a milk pail.

MARIJKE: Here. Take your holy milk.

EMMA: Marijke.

MARIJKE: Look down your nose at me, like your legs couldn't be pried open by Rudy Valentino!

EMMA: Marijke, I…I didn't know what to do. You had a boyfriend who was a German soldier. The whole town knew.

MARIJKE: Oh, really? Your fiancé gets hauled off to work in Germany. When's he coming back home? Whoops, there's another fella! And isn't he handsome in uniform—and so well fed, with that big gun slung over his shoulder. Bet he's a beast in the sack.

EMMA: They're our liberators, not our invaders.

MARIJKE: He takes orders. Carsten took orders too. The difference between you and me is that I actually loved Carsten. I wasn't, trying to squeeze everything I could from him.

EMMA: I wasn't—I didn't—

MARIJKE: I would have made a family with him. I'd still do it today. But Carsten died in the cold in Russia. And I couldn't even talk to anybody about it. Not even to you.

So I don't care anymore. When they came for me on Liberation Day I didn't scream or kick like the other girls. You saw it—I didn't care when the shears bit through to my scalp, and I didn't care when they painted the tar on over the bleeding. And that smug baker Bezuijen shoving my head down on the pavement, smiling and guilty—all those years he sold bread at a discount to the German officers. Nobody could go after him. But they sure as hell could go after me.

I don't care. I'm getting out.

EMMA: Marijke, I'm sorry.

MARIJKE: What are you sorry for? You reap what you sow, right?

EMMA: Please.

MARIJKE: What.

EMMA: I need help.

MARIJKE: Well good luck finding it. I sure coulda used some on Liberation Day.

She turns to leave.

EMMA: Marijke, I'm pregnant.

Pause.

MARIJKE: Well, it's not Jan's now is it.

EMMA: I need your help. I need you to help me know what to do.

MARIJKE: Give me one good reason why I should.

EMMA: I don't have one. Marijke, I'm sorry.

Pause. She considers.

MARIJKE: All right. I'll help you. But not for free. Do you have any money?

EMMA begins to cry.

EMMA: I don't. I don't have any money. I'm a mess. I'm so… unprepared for all of this.

MARIJKE: OK. First thing, no more crying. Oh jeetje[10], you are knocked up. What about Jan?

EMMA: I can't, I can't.

EMMA cries more.

MARIJKE: Verdikkeme nog en toe[11]!

So, this boy, your army boy. He's the father, right?

EMMA: Of course!

MARIJKE: Don't get upset! He's young. He's really, really young.

EMMA: I know! Believe me, I know!

MARIJKE: Is he good to you?

EMMA: Yes.

MARIJKE: Doesn't talk bad to you? Rough you up?

EMMA: No, never, not once.

MARIJKE: Does he know you're pregnant?

EMMA: I told him. He took off.

MARIJKE: Do you love him?

10 [Jeez]
11 [a milder version of "god damn it."]

Silence.

All right. What's so special about him.

EMMA: Something... happened. Right at the end when everything was at its worst. I saw him.

The scene shifts. Combat sounds. EMMA and AALTJE huddle in the shed, clinging to each other, terrorized. A huge explosion. The door blows in.

AALTJE: Emma!

AALTJE/
EMMA: Oh mijn God! Nee! Nee! Niet weer! Niet weer! [Oh my God! No! No! No more! No more!]

The smoke clears. ALEX is revealed, huddled up by the wall with his rifle. He's not shooting but he's definitely hunting.

EMMA: The smoke cleared and there was Alex! He was so... focused, he was, he was present. He was getting his job done. And then...

ALEX ducks below the wall and turns his head. They lock eyes across the stage. A moment. Then ALEX grins.

He grinned at me, in the middle of all of it. A big, toothy, goofy grin.

It was like he was saying...

ALEX: It's OK. Everything's going to be different now. It's going to be all right.

ALEX taps his helmet, climbs over the garden wall and disappears. We return to MARIJKE's house.

EMMA: And it was.

We were liberated.

MARIJKE: You know what you want to do. So do it. Easy.

EMMA: You think?

MARIJKE: Here's the deal. You marry him and sponsor my emigration.

EMMA: What does that mean?

MARIJKE: I'm a single woman. I can't emigrate without a sponsor. And nobody else around here is going to help me out, I guarantee you.

EMMA: Oh.

MARIJKE: You do this for me, and we're friends again. We're friends here, and we're friends in Canada. If you need me there, if this goes wrong, I'll be there. Yeah?

EMMA: Yeah.

MARIJKE: Now go find him. If it doesn't work out, come back and see me and we'll figure something else out. Go! Now!

EMMA: Thank you.

She exits.

Scene 7

CAVENDISH is in his underwear, his socks and his boots, holding a bloody towel to his ear. He dictates while checking his ear in a hand mirror. His uniform shirt and pants, also bloodied, hang over the back of his chair.

CAVENDISH: *(Dictating while ALEX types:)* Due to a shortage of barbers (comma) anyone having experience in this trade…ow!

ALEX: Once again, sir, I am so sorry.

CAVENDISH: Or the desire for training as a barber is asked to make application to RHQ stating qualifications and experience (period).

EMMA enters.

EMMA: Alex, I—

ALEX shares a look with CAVENDISH.

Oh! Oh! I'm very sorry. I'll go.

ALEX: Emma, wait!

CAVENDISH assesses the situation, then, resigned, grabs the towel and his uniform. He begins to leave, doubles back, and then:

CAVENDISH: *(Peevishly.)* P-r-o-p-h-y-l-a-x-i-s.

He exits.

ALEX: You're pregnant.

EMMA: Yes.

ALEX: You wouldn't lie to me about that, would you?

EMMA: No.

ALEX: 'Cause I can't do that any more. I can't. You have to tell me everything.

EMMA: I don't know if I can…say it good.

ALEX: Might as well give it a shot. What the heck.

EMMA paces, gathering her thoughts.

EMMA: Jan is my verloofde[12]. We are going to get married.

Before we are going to get married. But he goes away two years ago. And I don't know if he is dead or if he is alive, and while he is gone my father is dead and my brother is dead, and…

12 [Fiancé]

ALEX: And now he's back and—

EMMA: But he's is different… And you…but…

She struggles.

Something…but I can't tell you in English! I don't find the words.

ALEX: Say it.

EMMA: Weet je—wij hebben hier al heel, heel lang gewoont. Als ik met jou mee ga, zal alles veranderen. Niet alleen voor mij. Alles veranderd.

[But you know, we have been here for a long, long time. And if I go with you, all of that changes. I'll never come back.]

En ik hoor hier te blijven. Ik hoor voor m'n moeder te zorgen, vooral nu. Ik hoor met Jan te trouwen, om met hem een leven optebouwen, om voor hem te zorgen, en om kinderen met hem te krijgen.

[And I'm supposed to stay here. I'm supposed to take care of my mother, especially now. And I'm supposed to be with Jan, and make a life with him and take care of him, and finally make some children with him. But…]

Ik weet dat het stom is. Maar ineens wil ik hier weg. Ik wil eindelijk m'n eigen leven bepalen. Ik wil mij niet meer zorg maken over wat m'n moeder erover denk, of de buren, of de kerk.

[I know it's stupid. But suddenly I want to leave all of this behind and just live my life. Not worry so much about what my friends will think and what my mother will think and what the people in the church will think.]

En jij. Jij bent goed en lief en eerlijk.

[And you. You're kind and gentle and honest.]

Jij hebt iets om voor terug te gaan, binnenin.

[You've got something to go back to, inside of you.]

Als ik jou aankijk… dan zie ik…

[When I look in your face… I see….]

She kisses him, deeply.

ALEX: I sure liked what you said.

OK, and ya gotta know that it was when I saw you, when I saw you in that doorway, that's, that's when it happened for me. The guys say it doesn't happen like that but…it happened like that. I gotta ask—

EMMA: Alex, I go with you, to Canada. OK?

ALEX: We didn't get to the marriage proposal.

EMMA: Alex, will you marry me?

ALEX: *(Hesitates, startled by this, then:)* OK, all right then, sure!

Scene 8

Outside EMMA's house. Night.

JAN: Emmie! Emmie! I need to talk to you! Come out Emmie, we need to talk. I'm not going anywhere until you do!

The door opens—it's AALTJE instead.

AALTJE: Doe normaal, jongen[13]! Why are you hooting outside the house like some kind of fishwife?

JAN: I need to talk to Emmie.

13 [Act normal, boy!]

AALTJE: Well, she's not here.

JAN: I'll kill him.

AALTJE: You're not going to do anything.

JAN: I'll tear him apart, that little runt.

AALTJE: OK, simmer down, you. Jeetje[14], you've been into it, haven't you? Phew! Jenever! Where in the heck did you find Jenever!

JAN: My dad has a bottle. Hallelujah.

AALTJE: Oh yeah?

JAN: Had a bottle. Oh yeah. Hallelujah.

AALTJE: All right, stinky. You're in no shape to talk to my daughter, even if she were here. Do yourself a favour and sit on the steps for a while.

JAN: I gotta, I gotta—

AALTJE: No, sit, sit, SIT down.

JAN: Yes, ma'am.

He does so, heavily.

AALTJE: What a mess. Gimme that.

She swigs the last gulp of the bottle.

JAN: It's cold.

AALTJE: Because you're in nothing but shirtsleeves. It's almost autumn, stommert[15].

She goes inside, and comes out with a cardigan.

Put this on before you get pneumonia and die. Wouldn't that be funny—killed by a sniffle after walking halfway across Europe to get home.

---

14 [Jeez]
15 [Dummy]

JAN: I wish I was dead.

AALTJE: Don't be stupid, boy. What a catch—suicidal and grey as a mule.

JAN: It's not my fault!

AALTJE: I know! Who knows the things that come out of my mouth. Sometimes I just watch myself talking like I'm outside of my own body.

JAN: Why don't I feel like a human being anymore.

AALTJE: Aw, it's Hitler's fault. Everything's Hitler's fault. That'll do.

JAN: Hitler's dead. What do we do now?

Pause.

AALTJE: I don't really know. Roelof's dead. Anton's dead. My daughter hates me and the kale went to seed. I would blame the Lord but that's not going to do much good either. I need all the allies I can get these days.

She'll come around.

JAN: You think so?

AALTJE: She's a good girl. Everybody's just 'n beetje gek[16] right now. It'll all even out.

Go home, jongen[17]. Have a glass of water and then go to bed. You'll feel better in the morning.

JAN wanders off. AALTJE exhales. EMMA appears in the doorway.

EMMA: Thank you.

AALTJE: I don't like lying for you.

16 [A little bit crazy]
17 [Boy]

EMMA: I just…couldn't. Not tonight.

AALTJE: He knows what you've been up to. Everybody does. And he still wants you. You think about that.

AALTJE gets up, about to head back into the house.

EMMA: Moe. Moeder.

AALTJE: Laundry's not gonna fold itself—

EMMA: I'm going to marry Alex and go with him to Canada.

Silence.

I think we can have the wedding in a month or so, before he goes home. I'm hoping that you can help me with a dress.

Silence.

We can have the ceremony in the church—Alex's commanding officer will vouch for him to the Dominee.

Silence.

I know you don't like this. But I can't stay here anymore.

Silence.

Oh you're impossible! Can you not muster one word?

Silence.

Have it your way. I'll be out of your hair in a few months, as soon as the paperwork goes through. Then you can live your life the way you want it.

AALTJE: My second cousin Albert—he moved to Canada before the war. He ended up with his six kids living in a chicken coop with an outhouse. It's a wasteland there.

EMMA: I've seen pictures of Alex's farmhouse. It's very nice.

AALTJE: He's lying to you. He'll put you in a brothel.

EMMA: Moe do you even listen to yourself?

AALTJE: You don't know this man. You don't know his family, you don't know his people. They left us, Emmie! They left us to starve until the very end of the war! Those Canadian rotzakken[18], they didn't even bother. What makes you think he's going to take care of you?

EMMA: Moe, I'm pregnant.

AALTJE begins to cry.

Aw Moe… Moe, don't.

AALTJE: Oh go away! Go away!

EMMA: Please don't cry, Moe. I can't bear it!

AALTJE: And why shouldn't I? Think I'm made of stone? What about me?

She exits.

EMMA: Moe?

18 [Bastards]

Scene 9

Darkness. CAVENDISH's office. A figure stands in the dark by the gramophone, as at the beginning of the play. Beethoven plays, but this time something much more melancholy—String Quartet No. 14 in C-Sharp Minor, Op. 131: VI. Adagio Quasi un Poco Andante.

A few beats, then CAVENDISH enters, still in the dark.

CAVENDISH: Hello? Who's there?

DOMINEE: *(From the gramophone.)* Mr. Cavendish. *(He lifts the needle.)*

CAVENDISH: Dominee?

DOMINEE: I beg your pardon for the intrusion.

CAVENDISH: How did you get in here?

DOMINEE: I walked through the gate.

CAVENDISH: Did…did anyone say anything to you? You know, "halt" or something?

DOMINEE: I think he was asleep.

CAVENDISH: That's very comforting.

DOMINEE: I'd like to speak with you—

CAVENDISH: So you can just walk right in, then, can't you. Nobody stopping you. Play my records. Honestly. You people.

A little gratitude maybe. Is that too much to ask? "Hey, thanks for getting rid of the Germans for us. Sure do appreciate it."

DOMINEE: I'm sorry, Mr. Cavendish.

CAVENDISH: Well let's put some light on at least, if we're going to have a conversation. I'm just trying to finish my job with some sense of military decorum.

The lights switch on. CAVENDISH is dressed in a skirt and a gingham shirt tied up in front. He wears a crude blonde yarn wig.

DOMINEE: Good heavens!

CAVENDISH: Oh yes, right.

DOMINEE: Mr. Cavendish! What is the meaning of this... this...

CAVENDISH: Abomination?

DOMINEE: That might be the word!

CAVENDISH: It's for a play, all right? The men put on a play in the town hall this evening.

DOMINEE: What kind of play?

CAVENDISH: *L'il Abner.*

DOMINEE: From the comic strip?

CAVENDISH takes off the wig.

CAVENDISH: No one else wanted to be Daisy May. I was trying to be a good sport—nothing like something dramatical to keep the boys' minds off sex.

DOMINEE: I do not think it will have the desired effect.

CAVENDISH: Sir, why are you here?

Pause.

DOMINEE: While it is my hope that in times of trouble the members of my congregation can turn to me...but when you are the Dominee... Strangely, you are the only person in town I can talk to.

And I know you won't tell anyone in town about my troubles. Your Dutch is just terrible.

CAVENDISH: Please, sit down. Can I offer you anything? A cup of tea?

DOMINEE: Do you have…Canadian Club rye whisky?

CAVENDISH: Oh!

DOMINEE: My son has relieved me of all of my gin.

CAVENDISH pours a drink for the DOMINEE and for himself.

Do you have any children, Mr. Cavendish?

CAVENDISH: No sir, I can't say that I've found the opportunity for a family.

DOMINEE: My son Jan has been the joy of my life. When they took him away to Germany I felt I would lose my mind. We used to argue philosophy until late in the night, not as father and son, but as friends! But he is home now. And he is…I don't know what he is. He hates me. His fiancée has given up on him. And he has given up on God. He's my own son!

(He drinks.) Oh my. That's good.

You and my son are close to the same age. Who were you before the war?

CAVENDISH: That is a very good question.

They drain their glasses. He fills them again.

Alex, my clerk. He's 22. He seems so resilient. He'll go back to the farm or wherever he wants to go and just start over.

DOMINEE: I believe your young clerk is the man who has… attracted Jan's fiancée.

CAVENDISH: Oh—I hadn't— *(Putting it together.)* How awkward.

DOMINEE: But I also think Jan's troubles are greater than Emma.

CAVENDISH: If it helps, sir, I see Alex with that young woman and I think 'that's a new thing.'

Those records were left by my German predecessor. May I?

CAVENDISH puts the record back on.

All the documents they burned in the courtyard before they abandoned this house. They stole most of the furniture too. But he left the records and the gramophone with a note, written in English. Immaculate penmanship. It said "There is beauty still."

They listen for a bit.

DOMINEE: Beauty doesn't seem to be the right word.

CAVENDISH: No, you're right. Not this part. The Adagio is a catastrophe.

DOMINEE: I wonder what would we know about Beethoven if we could hear his whole body of work at once. All of the catastrophes and all of the odes to joy at the same time. Maybe that's how God hears the world. The whole stack of records instead of just one groove at a time.

CAVENDISH: It would be a cacophony.

DOMINEE: It certainly is.

They listen.

Scene 10

Video montage, or perhaps news clips. Canadian men marrying Dutch women. These carry on throughout the wedding sequence.

The church. ALEX and EMMA. She enters, veiled. The DOMINEE, in his robes, doing the honours. MARIJKE stands beside EMMA. AALTJE is absent.

The ceremony proceeds in dumb show, but when EMMA takes off her veil, MARIJKE turns around and addresses the audience. The ceremony continues to take place behind her, under this speech:

MARIJKE: One thousand years ago when my village first became a village, it was the dark ages. People believed one thing, or at least they said they all believed one thing. This church was made eight hundred years ago. My mother and my grandmother and my great-grand mother and my great-great-grand mother all got married in this church. And probably a whole lot of great greats before that, too.

DOMINEE: The text is from Isaiah:

"Forget the former things;
do not dwell on the past.
See, I am doing a new thing!
Now it springs up; do you not perceive it?
I am making a way in the wilderness
and streams in the wasteland."

MARIJKE: If Emma has a daughter, I wonder where she'll get married?

DOMINEE: And may the Lord bless you and keep you. May He make His face to shine upon you and be gracious unto you. May He lift up his countenance toward you...and give you peace. Amen.

ALL: Amen.

Scene 11

Transition (which may begin under the DOMINEE's benediction above): Video of men boarding boats, returning to Canada.

EMMA stands in travelling clothes. She holds two bags.

MARIJKE observes from a distance.

EMMA: Moe. That's it. I washed my bedding. It should be dry by the afternoon. There's a pile of things going to the Red Cross by the back door.

Everything fits into two bags now.

Silence.

I'll write to you from Canada. If I don't hear back from you…I…I'll just stop writing, all right?

Silence.

OK. I'm going.

AALTJE: You're pregnant. That's the first spark of good news I've had in five years. In this world as it is, that's a miracle! But you're going.

EMMA: Moe, everybody's poor. Everything's destroyed. Everybody's sad.

AALTJE: No! This is not how it's supposed to go.

EMMA: And how is it supposed to go? You want everything to be zoals het hoort[19]—coffee and cookies three times a day. Knitting by the stove with the radio on. You've still got his sweater.

AALTJE: No, I don't! I gave it to your fiancé. Remember him? Some things you're supposed to do! Your father and I—a family—we made a family here. We

19 [As it should be]

worked hard at it, even when we were poor, even when there was trouble, even when we were sad. We're sad, boo hoo! So what.

When your dad proposed I saw it, clear as day. Grandchildren, great-grandchildren. With dad by my side, right here, smoking his pipe! And when we get old and sick you and Anton are here to take care of us. We took care of you, for years and years! That's how it goes! You didn't live up to your part of the bargain!

EMMA: Moe, I can't… I can't stand it that you're like this.

AALTJE: Canada is the other side of the world, Emmie. I'll never see you again.

EMMA: Then come with me.

AALTJE: Am I supposed to tag along, some little slip of a mother-in-law living out of a cold back room, trying not to get in the way, being…chased around by coyotes? Or what else? Find a new Canadian husband like you? Hike my skirts and show my legs and let them leer at me? I'm fifty-three, Emmie.

EMMA: I'm sorry, Moe. I'm going.

AALTJE grabs EMMA, suddenly, and holds her tightly, desperately, for a long time, then snaps out of the room.

MARIJKE: Emma's mother didn't come to the jeep to see her off. Neither did my parents. And as we drove away through town we said goodbye.

EMMA: Goodbye little village.

MARIJKE: Goodbye church.

EMMA: Goodbye, Jan.

MARIJKE: Goodbye grocer.

EMMA: Goodbye, Va.

MARIJKE: Goodbye school.

EMMA: Goodbye, Anton.

MARIJKE: Goodbye bridge.

EMMA: Goodbye, Moe. Goodbye forever.

A video montage of emigration—departures, arrivals, Pier 21 in Halifax.

MARIJKE: We went to Amsterdam first—seven hours by jeep. Overnight at a women's hostel and then over the channel by ferry from Hoek van Holland the next morning. England. London. And then we took the train to Liverpool and headed out to sea. Emma and me on the Queen Elizabeth.

It took six days to cross to Halifax. When Emma slept I climbed up onto deck and held onto the railings and listened to the water and just... *(She breathes in and out.)*

At Halifax we got on the train. Three days past forests and lakes to Sudbury, which was my stop. Right in the middle of the country.

They cling to each other.

You're gonna be fine. You're gonna be great. Write me.

EMMA: I will. Write me.

MARIJKE: I will. I'll come visit you and the cowpokes as soon as I can.

EMMA: You can always stay with me if you need to.

MARIJKE: Come on. You got great big things to go to. And I'm terrific! I mean, how hard can it be? Nobody's shooting, nobody's starving. *(She snaps her fingers.)*

"Piece of cake."

Goodbye, Emma.

EMMA: Goodbye, Marijke.

MARIJKE steps aside.

MARIJKE: And then two more days by herself, past more forests and lakes then white fields and white fields and white fields.

And then one day.

EMMA steps out onto the platform. She searches the crowd. ALEX steps out from the wing. He's been waiting for her train, in civilian clothes.

EMMA: Hi.

ALEX: Hi.

EMMA: I missed you.

ALEX: I missed you.

MARIJKE: I have no idea what happens next. Isn't that exciting?

The End.